Still Falling

Also by Jennifer Grotz

POETRY

Cusp

The Needle

Window Left Open

TRANSLATION

Psalms of All My Days by Patrice de La Tour du Pin

Rochester Knockings by Hubert Haddad

Everything I Don't Know by Jerzy Ficowski
(with Piotr Sommer)

Still Falling

POEMS

Jennifer Grotz

GRAYWOLF PRESS

This publication is made possible, in part, by the voters of Minnesota through a Minnesota State Arts Board Operating Support grant, thanks to a legislative appropriation from the arts and cultural heritage fund. Significant support has also been provided by the McKnight Foundation, the Lannan Foundation, the Amazon Literary Partnership, and other generous contributions from foundations, corporations, and individuals. To these organizations and individuals we offer our heartfelt thanks.

Published by Graywolf Press
212 Third Avenue North, Suite 485
Minneapolis, Minnesota 55401

All rights reserved.

www.graywolfpress.org

Published in the United States of America

ISBN 978-1-64445-231-8 (paperback)
ISBN 978-1-64445-232-5 (ebook)

2 4 6 8 9 7 5 3 1
First Graywolf Printing, 2023

Library of Congress Control Number: 2022946144

Cover design: Jeenee Lee

Cover art: Caravaggio, *The Conversion on the Way to Damascus*

to Adam Zagajewski

I w śmierci będziemy żyli,
tylko inaczej

Contents

Still Falling

Staring into the Sun

What had been treacherous the first time
had become second nature, releasing
the emergency brake, then rolling backward
in little bursts, braking the whole way down
the long steep drive. Back then,
we lived on the top of a hill.

I was leaving—the thing we both knew
and didn't speak of all summer. While you
were at work, I built a brown skyline of boxes,
sealed them with a roll of tape
that made an incessant ripping sound.
We were cheerful at dinner and unusually kind.
At night we slept under a single sheet,
our bodies a furnace if curled together.

It was July. I could feel my pupils contract
when I went outside. Back then,
I thought only about how you
wouldn't come with me. Now I consider
what it took for you to help me go.
On that last day. When I stood
in a wrinkled dress with aching arms.
When there was only your mouth at my ear
whispering to get in the truck, then wait
until I was calm enough to turn the key.

Only then did we know. How it felt
to have loved to the end, and then past the very end.

What did you do, left up there in the empty house?
I don't know why. I don't know
how we keep living in a world
that never explains why.

Medium

In the nineteenth century,
I'd have found a medium,
a knocking table, a crystal ball,

but to conjure him now
I go online and Google,
scroll page after page until

his name disappears
in a list of random links,
but still there's his handle on Skype,

still the picture of him crossing the finish line
of the Portland Marathon,
still the smiling-in-the-wind-on-the-beach photo, still

that email that arrived at 3 a.m.
back in February, those words of such
love and affirmation out of the blue

that I knew were strange but didn't query,
thought maybe he'd been up drinking,
was feeling sentimental, and

that must have been
the night of the first attempt
we found written in his journal,

when he'd thrown himself off a bridge
into the cold, dirty Willamette
but survived,

and how disappointed
he must have felt then,
the body involuntarily countering

with a surge of adrenaline,
his body feeling at its
utmost alive.

iPoem

Now there are mini-moons, I read,
primordial crumbs. Or rather
there always were but now our instruments
are sensitive enough to register.

It probably means I'm dead. Or dying.
How I spend all day staring into a screen,
or typing, or reloading. Not a mirror, not a window,
a screen I hold in my hand, endlessly reach for,

sleep next to. Photogenic instead of
poetogenic: I like to think
the poem's resistance to be about you
is poetry's critique of you

and of how I cling to you
as though you were the world.

Now I See through a Glass Darkly

Frozen, melted, refrozen, the dull gray dark
lurking inside it, bubbles entrapped and
opaque cataracts with translucent edges.
It fascinates too much: watching the river freeze,

it starts along the banks, the reeds
frozen upright and ice scalloping each side,
slowly reaching toward the center, like fingers
covering eyes, the river slowly going blind.

Looking up through the river's narrow eye,
surely the sky is too hard to see. As is, looking down,
what's beneath the surface. But I can see
frozen panes of ice float by, some thin as

drenched napkins or sheets of tissue
that collide with driftwood
with no tear but a shatter, a friable
crash. Why does it fascinate so?

More and more I pay attention to what's not there.
Not there or in the dark. I don't want to be
certain. Don't let me see. Whatever I see—
either the world is broken or I am.

This Living Hand

To open the heavy glass door required
a three-second pause to pull hard enough
to unseal the vacuum of thick rubber
keeping out the cold. Which is how I spotted them
in February on the ground, the french fries
some student likely spilled or threw out
on the way to class. That entire semester,
every week, for three seconds, I'd look down
and find them, like human fingers gone pallid,
rolled in dirt, buried in or commingling with
the decomposing leaves. But they never
did. No one picked them up but the wind,
which eddied them over time into a little pile.
Snow covered them, then melted in the spring,
leaving them intact. Their stubborn composition
disgusted, then fascinated, then bewildered me.
I took pictures, the way Monet painted haystacks.
By semester's end, I stopped believing it sensical
for poets to yearn for immortality through verse.

November

Even when the grapes were still green and firm,
the vines had grown heavy, charged with fruit.
Then sun-kindled, they made the subtle switch

to tawny purple and started to soften.
The mouth softens thinking of them,
and the whole backyard smells now of grape and

grapes starting to ferment because of those that fell
that make a sticky mush over which hover
thirsty bees. My neck aches from

looking up at the pendulous clusters,
holding each clump in one hand to clip
its stem with the other, and they

settle into my palm or spill fat purple drops
that disappear like bruise-colored marbles in the grass.
The squirrel balanced on the fence post

holds a filched grape in his paws,
rolling it like a little crystal ball, nervous,
then looks up, then changes from necromancer

to nibbler, eating it hurriedly,
knowing he's being observed, then
freezes when he catches my gaze.

Why are you in such a hurry? I want to say,
it's November, penultimate month,
when fingers are coldest, ungloved

and wet from the rain slicking off
the grapevines still waiting to be gleaned.
It's time to savor. We're penultimate, too.

Come, No Longer Unthinkable

Like someone who puts out the light
the better to see into the dark, look,
I put it out.

Then the dark changes, it becomes
various things instead of one. That's
what lures me out

among the slick, black trunks of pines,
soft from drinking up the melted snow.
Uniform and tall as bars,

the forest is the only cage I've entered
to be free. Under moonlight, ice light,
the deer nose in gold spokes of grass,

piercing the stiff snow, glossy as meringue,
with their perfect hooves. They brave
the center, unlike the milkweed

orbiting the clearing that look like
all the different phases of the moon, I thought,
fanned out for display. Did I think it or did I

mind it? Because the mind won't stop minding.
Or the eye stop eyeing. That's why, closer up,
the milkweed's eyeing, too: a cottony globe

in its socket looks out from the hood
of a wood-gray eyelid. I stare—the dark
requires staring to be sure—at what

it's staring down at, too: a stone, and beneath it,
a patch of wet earth. Where one can't see
any further, only imagine. Where

darkness is just
a purgatory of things unseen.
I stand right there, in that particular dark.

The Crows

There must have been greetings
that rhymed with each of them,

but now she only remembers
the goodbyes, the countless times

they stood together speechless
under a starry meal of snow,

crows congregating above them
in bare winter branches, all through

the desperate sadness at the end,
one of them still madly in love

while the other admitted defeat,
taking turns as if exchanging

a heavy suitcase. They were, after all,
always traveling. Somehow never at home.

He loved her in libraries and parking lots,
in cemeteries and cafés. She loved him

in the held breath of elevators, in stairwells
and trains. He loved her in daylight. But also

in the dark. She loved him most at the end
of the day, telling a story at dinner

while waving his fork and knife. He was her
never husband and she his never wife.

There must have been greetings
that rhymed with each of them.

All along, though they couldn't hear it,
before they had stopped being lovers,

before they had even started,
back when they were two people leaving

a restaurant in summer's dusk,
the crows were growing busy, numerous,

there was one coming to land
on every branch of every tree, once

the thumbless black hands of their wings
had finished stroking the malleable sky,

all along, though they couldn't hear it,
the birds had been winging

their silent applause
for the love that was going to be, then was.

December

Entering the forest at night,
able to see the next few steps

but not what's after that—something
in me resists, something else draws

forward, and fresh snow illuminates
the path to follow, though the deer

move discursively through the trees.
It is not sad, this walking, it

is marvelous, the chilly wetness
on the cheeks is snow. Somehow

it always comes back to winter,
it comes back to these tentative steps

taken under a blue moon
through a white cathedral of trees,

while something in me resists,
something else enters the wild.

Heading There

I will call desert this kingdom that you were,
sun this loneliness. I will say
wasp to name the fear. When night falls,
I will call what haunts this landscape bat. Sky

will be the word for having known all along.
You dreaded the sky, how it hung
over death, but dying, that's
the country you loved. I am headed there,

but I am taking the sorriest roads. I am
destroying your face, your hands,
the smell of your sweat. I am your
enemy, and I will behave like an enemy,

I will love you so much I erase you,
I will call desert the kingdom that you were.

She Kept All These Things and
Pondered Them in Her Heart

1.

Pondered, it rhymes with wondered,
which she also did, it means
weighed, also

2.

it hurts, heavy treasure piled inside
the chest, heaving, what made it so?
Everyone being gone,

3.

no one left to remember,
to face it. And have you tried to face it? No,
it doesn't have a face, if it had a face

4.

you would have slapped it hard—
Don't ask what is it. You already know. Let it be
the wind. I pledge allegiance to the wind,

5.

to the tumbleweed in which it rolls, to a herd of them
roaming the arid plains, head down as if foraging, but really
disintegrating bit by bit to release the seed within—

6.

Does a tumbleweed have a face? No,
and I didn't face it, I pondered it, kept it like
a bag of coins that one day I would weigh and count:

7.

ponder the mystery of his pain, the harm he did to others,
ponder the places we grew up, the dust, the loop
of highway I'd drive at night, circling and circling

8.

while time was running out.
While tumbleweeds scuttled across to interrupt
the highway's thought—then became the thought.

9.

There is more and more I tell no one.
There is more and more I let the wind blow away.

Incantation

I know that to find you I will
have to leave the earth and go out,

as I left my lamplit room
and its clicking electric baseboards

to enter this wood quivering with beeches
and wild turkeys and cereal-colored leaves,

have to leave my life
that has become so small and inevitable

and my gratitude that gets chiseled down
and grows back again,

into the stillness, the windless calm,
into such loneliness, the blue sky,

the heartbreak indigo, undifferentiated
as darkness, untouchable, unarrivable,

traveling through it, then simply not,
into the nowhere, the no more,

the imagination. Down here is where
I lost you, somewhere beneath

low-swinging stoplights and the desert's
granulated sunset that settled

in one's eyes and hair, sunset
you could taste from the wind

carrying smells of the stockyard,
and the ground pushing up the sharp

fluorite rocks that cut our tanned legs,
that palimpsest of a landscape,

every return depositing or wiping clear
another memory of that street we

so desolately wandered, oh my lost little brother,
I will look until I find you.

January

At first, like grief, the snow
covers everything. Then it begins to reveal
the wan and sickly rainbow of our presence,
cinnamon-sugar of boot-worn paths, dog urine,
roads rimmed with black exhaust. Or
in the woods carpeted with new snow,
ground threatens to give, unstable ice
creaking like floorboards below.
Winter necessitates looking down.

World winnowed down to whites and grays
and branches blown bare: this is just my mind
of winter, I thought. Depression, it is said,
is gross indifference to the world. But
I wasn't indifferent, I was sinking.

I stared at nothing and heard my voice say,
just wait a little longer. I didn't know
which was me—the urging or the sinking.
Outside the window, decidedly silver
and patient, it seemed to me, moonlight
took its time filtering down through the trees.

The Morning Will Be Bright, and Wrong

While thinking of Adam's death, she hears about Jon's,
just last week, an old flame, the composer. Their ending
so painful that a decade later, when buying her new home,
she wavered because it was by a street with his last name
and wasn't sure she could stomach walking by
that name every day. Which is what she does now
to take in the news, take a walk, it's what she did
when Adam died, end of last winter. It's what
she did when Josh died, too, that holiday weekend,
everyone out of town, so much ice on the sidewalk
no choice but to walk in the middle of the road,
using her red scarf as a tissue, ice caking her lashes.

It's blinding outside and the snow's a canvas
soaking up pigments mixed by the sun, blues, purples,
yellows, pinks and orange. The sun dazzles
the melting stalactites studding the rooftops.

                                    It was
a nearly perfect affair, they worked in the mornings,
she drank too much coffee and let a cigarette burn so long
its ash would spill onto the page and that was
one happiness. Another was late afternoons
when she'd join him in bed, and then after, it would be
time for an aperitif and they'd cook dinner, eat,
discuss their days. Some nights he'd go back to the piano
and play Scarlatti while she stood behind him with her arms
around his shoulders light enough, she imagined,
not to hinder his playing. Still it ended badly, suddenly,
irrevocably.

It's the same walk she takes each time,
from her house to Brooks Street, Brooks to the Genesee,
then along the river until it meets the Erie Canal, then
under the highway, then into the forest unless
the little alarm of fear sounds in her, it often does,
a woman alone. The day she learned about Adam,
she'd stopped on the bridge crossing the river
to take out her phone for a photo, saw the text.

She could find another walk, but she doesn't want to,
she doesn't want to get in the car to avoid the walk,
avoid the death, avoid the river. This is the walk
by her house, by the street with Jon's name, it's
the walk along the river that's hazel-green in summer,
silver-blue in spring, frozen sometimes in winter.
A walk is a poem. So is a grief.

When she gets home, the snow on her boots smears
like paint on the doormat. She finds the cats asleep
on the table they're supposed to stay off of,
the patch of light they always seek makes their warm fur
gleam. There's a word for it, she just read it today, *apricity*,
recorded by Cockeram in 1623, "the warmeness
of the Sunne in Winter," now obsolete.

March

Everything was moving, pixilated, snow
splintering down and nestling in the yellow grass.
March: a constant darting in the corner of my eyes,
time of year the world wants us to look
several places at once. And smell: mixture of hay and mud,
sunlight on straw, and not a scent but a tickle
in the nose while brushing the horse
to help him shed his winter coat, hair falling
in wisps and clumps, inciting the barn swallows'
deft descents from the rafters to pick up
a blade of straw, a beakful of hair
for weaving a nest that will be soft and warm.
All winter the horse had paid closer attention to me
than any human. When I rode him bareback,
all I had to do was look
where I wanted to go and he could sense
from my seat all the way up my back
the slight direction my neck had turned.
He weighed 953 pounds. To make him stop,
all I had to do was hold my breath.

May

Early morning frost—a field of full-blown dandelions
furred with ice, stiff and voluptuous as firework explosions.
And a flying jewelry of insects and birds.
Along the roadside, sprays of wild carrot and chicory
hover disembodied from their stalks, or so they appear
as my car whizzes past. Days blinded with light,
leaf shadows pouring across the windshield
like a liquefaction of lace. It's May, and
the run-over skunk by the rural dance school
has all the little ballerinas gagging. I park
under the sign for the Golden Dynasty,
the Chinese place in the strip mall, and see words
are how we make ourselves at home. Or where:
birds are nesting in the hollow of each vowel.

Poem or Story

Childhood was a story, a journey, it was a place
one had to leave. Whatever I read,

I wondered if it was a poem or a story.
My mother said it was a story if it had an ending.

But poems ended too, I thought. Or else
they were middles. A journey might be a story

where the ending is a place. I wondered
too much, and wondering was a kind of place, too,

somewhere in the middle. I had no memory
of the beginning. My life from its start

was an expanding middle, my mother's.
Was I a poem, then, or a story, was I

taking a journey? As a child, we dressed up
in our Sunday clothes when we flew on a plane.

If traveling with our parents, we sat in the back
so mother could smoke. A cigarette was a story

that ended when a little pile of ash had
mostly landed in the lidded metal box

embedded in the armrest mother and I shared.
She'd send me into the convenience store

to fetch a pack, Benson & Hedges Ultra Lights
Menthol 100s, and candy cigarettes for me.

Chalky white with hot-pink tips.
I carried them in a patent leather purse

next to my Avon lipstick samples and smoked them
when she smoked. And left a lipstick print

on one end like she did too. Smoking had a beginning
and an ending and a dreamy middle part

that was time passing. Other times,
if my brother and I flew on a plane alone,

they put us up front, once in first class, where
we were served a breaded chicken cutlet

on a gleaming ceramic plate. When I cut into it,
melted herb butter pooled from its middle.

As if it were a poem, I thought.
The flight attendant called it chicken Kiev.

Free Fall

She was in a coma, the doctor told me
over the phone, her electrolytes out of whack,
that was the literal, while I was on another continent,
standing on a cliff, looking down at the sublime
view my new friend had brought me to see, that
was literal too, the glittering sea, and the harbor
with tiny boats lined up like teeth. Below us,
cypresses jutted from the cliff's red rock.
I couldn't understand how a person,
a consciousness, was a kind of invention,
provisional, and could be erased by glucose
and potassium spilling through cell walls.
That was what I was thinking as we stood
in the small crowd that had gathered
to watch the sunset. I marveled
at the loss in store. Though I saw the beauty.
A sky stained every color but green. A slow,
liminal glower stretching flat and thin
as settling smoke, a horizon and a unit of time.
Let us go then, you and I, while she, I
shuddered, was a patient etherized upon a table.
Then I shuddered again as the man
standing next to us jumped
and fell and kept falling. Terror bloomed,
then his parachute. Then the literal and figurative
reordered, then what we'd reached for
instinctively in the moment of falling . . . then
wordlessly we let go of each other's hand.

Who Understands

« Oui, j'ai été mon père et j'ai été mon fils » —SAMUEL BECKETT

I was my mother and I was my child.
It wasn't a dream: I was the murderer
and the one who was killed, I was
the witness and also I looked away,
I told the truth and I was the one
who lied, who lied. I was a gun
and the bullet loaded inside it, the unseen
trajectory through air, I was
the flesh, the wall, the slab of wood
the bullet slowed to a stop inside of, then
I was numb and silent, then I was
the swiftest rain of shattered glass,
the bare feet in which the splinters lodged, sharp
pricks, I tried to walk away, I was trying
to walk away. I wanted to hide, or
I wanted attention, I was the frightened, anxious
human entering the woods, I was
the hundred anonymous animal eyes
surveilling the human who entered. Do
you understand? I was your mother
and also your child. I was the one
who was confused. You're
the one who understands.

Grief

Waking to cry, good grief, the morning after,
and the morning after that, loneliness crowded,
ignorance attentive, posthumous life, scrambling
eggs while crying, crying in the shower,
all the muddied thinking turned clear and pure,
time measured by a fly's return to be swatted
from the face, the arm. It was summer. Sweat
and warm rain, every single thing was a paradox,
a prayer. Was "something understood," said Herbert,
which conjured to me shelter, I stood under
something. Was it heaven? What did I understand?
World slowed down and broken and random and wrong:
I stood under nothing at all. Except memory,
how once, a summer morning years ago, I stood
over grass gleaming with dew and watched
countless tiny frogs leap like exclamations.

Before

Sweatpants balled up where his legs would be,
but otherwise just like the others parked in the hallway,
nodding to visitors. Next to him,
his best friend, obese and in a cowboy hat,
holding a chihuahua on his lap, and next
on his wheeled throne the hateful former pastor

my mother mockingly called King David,
who endlessly shouted *Help* then *Go to hell*
at anyone's approach. This was the gauntlet
I traversed to reach her, a bedlam
of beeping monitors, a bevy of abandoned
walkers shod with gouged tennis balls.

Now she's gone; are the others?
Surely there's still the faint mixture
of urine and bleach, an announcement overhead
bingo is about to begin. Surely the squeak
of nurses' shoes on beige linoleum, a cry
unheard and a pull cord stained with blood.

Before I'd have to leave, there was a silence
we'd hold together. Her eyes would scan
the windowpane for the doe with a broken leg
we'd watched all that winter
limp out sometimes from the naked trees.
We studied her for clues when she appeared

and made the silence with our held breath
lengthen the glimpse. It lasted until
it had to end, like an embrace. Then I would
make my way back out, the bingo announcer's
shout, *B-4*, and a woman staring down at
her card slowly repeating it aloud.

Greens and Purples

They don't make a sound. Neither does my staring.
Just throw a skin of bread into the water and see:

the large fish rise from the dark to tear off little bites
while smelt scatter like a shattered alphabet.

Watch as the fisherman pulls up his mustard-colored nets,
then, like the mind obsessing over a confusion, a wrong, a guilt,

he beats the freshly caught octopus against the rocks.
Forty times at least, he says, to tenderize it.

Say something true but not despairing, I told myself.
That was how I chose silence or it chose me.

To be by water is a kind of waiting, something
eternally incomplete. If I watch long enough,

the sea is all green and purple, I can see it
as the ancient Greeks did, who had no word for blue.

Sometimes I could say things before I felt them. Sometimes
by the time I felt, the words were already gone.

I have become too interested in silence. It is like
finding the single position that causes no pain.

And the end isn't silent, it's when
everyone starts speaking in different languages.

That's what God does when we get too proud.
He makes us lonely.

Go Along

   —return to Cassis

That far-off glittering that leaps right off the sea
into the sky is the gulls, at dusk, fishing.
And that happy excess of landing back
in another language is the temporary doubling
of the world that has two words for everything,

starting with the gulls, *les goélands*,
it sounds like go along, which they do, just above
the smeary sea spreading itself flatter and flatter.
Yes: something about how flat it is, and blue,
except when it's gray and like a liquid steel,

the sea makes me want to go along,
the lapping waves calm the mind
though the sea is the quintessence
of violence and force just distantly removed.
Sometimes the waves look like sharks,

sometimes they look like swords or spears
or soldiers in a cacophony of war,
which make the *goélands* conjure white
handkerchiefs madly waving surrender.
The sea teases out these meditations,

though other times it returns each thing
to what it is, the unorganized slosh or
slap against the pier, the unsynchronized cries
of the gulls, the day's overwhelming sense of
loneliness which I can only register,

not do anything about—and the blue of it
is endless so I'll love it endlessly, it is
a treasure hoard of sardines gleaming like coins
beneath the surface, *goélands* above,
and I stare until I almost become one,

the wind's invisible muscles
whipping beneath my belly, I imagine the air's
damp ripples of velvet as I go along,
as I walk with arms in one language,
in another, stretch wings wide.

Marseille

July and the sound of cicadas is unceasing
as doubt or death or dust's bright splintering in the sun.
Along the Vieux Port, boats are raised on pulleys,
under which tanned men scrape down the hulls.
Urine drying on the hot sidewalk in the noon heat
mixes with the smell of fish, where the morning's catch
is spread on tables under umbrellas for sale.
Thank you for not urinating on the ground
the sign entering the boulodrome reads
because it's mostly men who play pétanque.
Often they stand so still with concentration
you can see the sun-bleached sand in their eyebrows,
sand a scirocco blew from Africa. Cigarette tucked
behind his ear, one player draws a circle in the dust
with his boot. Another swings a steel ball in one hand
and lets go. The smell of perspiration is holy, the sky
couldn't be more blue. Everyone spends a long time
looking at the ground. Bare earth, but slight shifts
in topography to consider, calibrations of pebble,
bulging tree roots. Sunlight is everywhere at once.
Look at their shadows, said the man who brought me
to teach me how to tell which ball was closer
to the bouchon. I look at the ground the way
I stare at the sea when a great ship floats on the horizon
from a distance I could never swim alone
until I perceive it's not fading away, it's fading
into being, in the time it takes to write this, it's here.

August

water and wind do it too
but differently
it is another thing to be

eroded by light

that's to be scintillated
then scorched
the STOP sign in the desert

stops being cherry

to be tomato-colored then
persimmon
by august it streaks

yellow blurs its letters

so much light
makes things dull
in color but

sharp in sensation

makes thorns needles
wild fire that leaves
a track of black stubble

and stumbles across

a highway
if the wind takes it
to the next field

it blinds differently than darkness

it tightens the pupils
it bleaches
the world away

The Conversion of Paul

—for Paul Otremba

Bewildered—something in me is made wild
from looking at it—but something
also chastened, subdued, because
it holds my gaze a long time. It is itself
a unit of time—one bewildering instant
caught by Caravaggio's imagination—Saul
thrown off his horse, landing on his back,
taken aback, Saul becoming Paul, struck blind,
being spoken to by the light. It seems
none of us really cares for Gunn's
take on the painting, defiant insistence
of being hardly enlightened, but I admire
the chiaroscuro-like contrast he makes
between Paul's wide-open arms
and the close-fisted prayers
of the old women he notices in the pews
when he turns away. But even if
Paul on the ground is still falling, both
are gestures of blind faith, as Stan calls
it. You call it a bar brawl, all this one-upmanship,
but in your poem you don't take sides,
you give your own perspective, twenty-first century,
postmodern, belated. You ask what happens if
a hundred people hold the painting in their minds
at the same time. Will it gain a collective dullness,
a tarry film like too much smoke? But I like to think
it would sharpen the focus, deepen the saturation
of the red cloak, crumpled like bed sheets, beneath him.
A lot could be made of how Gunn, then Stan, then you
make a poem out of a painting, but Caravaggio
did it first, making the painting out of verses

from the Bible. All art traffics in some kind of translation.
Which might be another word for conversion. God says,
Saul, Saul, why persecutest thou me? It is hard for thee
to kick against the pricks. Which makes me think
of the horse, who should be more visibly
shaken probably from such a flash of light.
No one seems to register how claustrophobic
it all is, difficult to believe it's happening
outside, where there should be space
for all this stretching out, and the horse
wouldn't have to raise one hoof so as not
to step on Paul. And the groomsman,
why isn't he doing anything but staring down?
Like all Caravaggios, it's sexual, the arms and legs
splayed as if ready to be taken by God himself,
but it's really an outsize gesture of shock.
I heard the news of your being sick, Paul,
when I was in Italy. If God himself
is the radiance that struck Saul into Paul,
then what is the darkness swimming around
everything? It makes one feel inside of something,
confined by such dark. Afterward, the Bible says,
Paul *was three days without sight, and*
neither did eat nor drink. Now after chemo,
you consume a thousand-calorie shake
called The Hulk to keep from losing weight.
I went to see the painting when I was in Rome
in September. It is a pleasure to look at a painting
over time. To consider it along with others,
including you, my friend, over decades.
Something in the painting is insistently
itself, intractable, and yet inexhaustible meaning

keeps also being revealed. Paul, thinking of you
when I look at the painting changes it. I see you
vulnerable, surrendered, beautiful and young,
registering that something in you has changed
and what happens next happens to you alone.
And inside you. Conversion is a form of being saved,
like chemo is a form of cure, but it looks to me
like punishment, a singling out, ominous,
and experienced in the dark. When
I used to see the painting, I was an anonymous
bystander. Now I am helpless. It is
and you are, in the original sense, awful.
I can't get inside the painting
like I suddenly and desperately want to,
to hold him, to help you get back up.
And now, for Paul, everything has changed.

For Patrick

It was that August you biked up the mountain
to pitch a tent on Treman lawn as if
you were Robert Lowell, though I was the one
having hallucinations that night the thermostat
broke in Cornwall Cottage and the furnace
pumped so much heat into my little room
I dreamt I was a roasted chicken, tossing
and turning to ensure I browned evenly
on all sides, until it stirred me out
of sleep and onto the floor, still too hot,
and finally made me drag a blanket
to the lawn to sleep one last hour
at the foot of your tent, the dew-slicked grass
felt like sliding into a shallow pool
with both a fever and a sunburn. How
we laughed the next day, delirious
with hangover and exhaustion. What had I
been thinking, that the literary world would
eat me alive? Which of us was driven more,
more full of yearning? I chased inspiration,
but half of it, you said, might be never
giving up, to never stop working. That,
it turned out, was right. The other half
would be finding someone to hash out
everything to do with poems, agreeing
and not, smoking late into the night, and then,
did you ever think? getting old enough
to bury friends and mentors, crying in the pew
just as we did that August on the porch before you
climbed back on your bike and rode back down
the mountain to the world, the work, the poems.

Over and Above

Because I didn't want it to end,
and because I was all alone again,
because in those seasons attention
was my only form of prayer,
I attended the summer rain.
When it pelted the lake like fingers
across a keyless piano, I attended
the fingertips' perforations on the soft surface.
Inside a theater of quiet the trees made,
permeable, though, at least studded
by bird song, I attended the mosquitos
floating like eyelashes in the thick air.
And before turning back from the lake's edge,
needing to confirm it still so,
I wrapped my hand around a cattail
and squeezed: spongy and veloured
as an espresso-soaked ladyfinger.
I grew in those seasons, said Thoreau,
like corn in the night. . . . They were
not time subtracted from my life, but so much
over and above my usual allowance.
Sometimes I imagined the rain was also
attending me, that I was its interlocutor.
It had been born, it seemed to say,
like any living thing, from certain
right conditions, it had gained force
as it grew and persisted to stay alive.
And the rain could pray harder
than me. It continued even when
I stopped listening, then started again.

That is how seconds, minutes, a whole
afternoon would spill out until there was neither
forward nor back only this other
kind of now, over and above, this thick
haze of humid heat gauzing the distant trees.

Rain

Sometimes I dream too vividly,
I go to be with my dead, I wake
and they're still alive in my mind
so I stay there; the longer I am here,
the more I shuttle back and forth, the harder
to say what living is. It's almost like reading:
the part your eyes read, and the part
you see in your mind. Right now

it's to be by an open window,
midnight in September, rain
falling in Warsaw, looking down from
a hotel room at a neighborhood
under renovation, shiny black roads
that invite your gaze, construction cranes
and whispering lindens. To exist on earth,
if you are lucky, is to be alone
then with loved ones, or with loved ones
and then alone, to walk streets among
strangers, to speak the language
or not, to stare for hours into a screen

that didn't exist in childhood, or, just now,
to feel cool wind twist around bare ankles,
rain echoing below, drops landing in
little claps, a steady, somnolent applause,
it is a sentence, a syntax that continues,
a spell of little letters, a voice,
a connection made with the beloved's eyes,
how that sustains, how it comforts, how
it prolongs one's longing, how it's almost
too simple to say. And too strange.

One recognizes it again
when it rains. It velvets the air.
What doesn't ever actually happen
is no small amount of being alive.

All the Little Clocks Wind Down

Now the blackberries in the yard
have finished their work of fattening with juice.
They wanted to flower, wrote Rilke, *but we*
wanted to ripen. That meant being dark
and taking pains. Whatever the freight
trains are carrying tonight is acrid, just
sulphurous, and looking out at the bay, dull
pewter, something feels over, it's all over,
elsewhere, even the wind. A place is just
a place, innocent, but the mind makes it
palimpsest, makes now go back to then.
I smoked a cigarette with him once on that corner,
the two of us laughing or starting a fight.
The two of us walking out of a movie theater
or into a bar. We sat so happily together
reading and not speaking at all, our arms or legs
touching without either of us looking up.
Tonight the waves arrive tremulous
as a small voice breaking, almost defeated,
that wants to be heard. The freight train interrupts
with its blur of furtive cargo. Darkness, my name
is Jennifer Grotz and I am almost ready to confess
I was reckless and careless and selfish
with my life. I am almost ready to see,
I am almost ready to close my eyes and do
what the darkness beckons, now that he
is like a poem read by no one, now that I am
like an illiterate desperate to understand,
now that she is like a moth's kiss on the pane
unfastening at my presence, now that

I stare at water, at cloud, at sky,
trying to see through to the other side.
For a good while it worked, this life
I made, these poems that made
wanting, not having, enough.

The Salt Mine

When my mind lingers too long in the dark,
I think of the salt mine at Wieliczka, built
eight hundred years ago a thousand feet
underground, and of the workers
who toiled there months and years at a time
by candlelight, who after hours carved chapels
so they could pray, salt-crystal chandeliers
to light them, who carved statues
of luminaries of their day, kings and queens,
popes and artists, Copernicus, Beethoven, Goethe,
and saints whose feet and hands are worn away now
from centuries of kissing, a project vaster
than any single life could complete, a cathedral
that commenced Gothic, then Renaissance,
and ended Baroque; I think how the human heart
is an underground labyrinth filled with chambers,
how history is murky, lopsided, and literally dissolving,
how a tour guide instructs visitors to lick the walls,
and most unbearable, I think of the horses
lowered in by harness, then bred below,
who trod in circles to work the pulleys
that raised and lowered baskets of supplies
from above, salt mined from below,
the beautiful horses who, while workers
chipped their stories onto every surface,
wordlessly spent their whole lives underground.

In Sicily

I had a vision once. Or rather a dream,
and in it I was flying. Awake, I was in Erice,
that is to say, already in the clouds,
the town perched so high on a mountain that
many mornings, if you stepped onto the balcony,
you'd be standing in white. You could sense
the cloud you were inside of moving.
But I was asleep when I took flight, swiftly rising
the way one might on a tall Ferris wheel,
the moment when the rising turns perilous,
the landscape growing small and soon to be
irretrievable, no brakes because there is no engine
but the mind that my will had to choke,
and so I woke and sat straight up in bed.

No one noticed my quiet terror
when I went downstairs and took my coffee
with the others. It was certain I had just averted
my life's end. The conversations of breakfast
were muted by the clinking of cups and spoons.
I thought of my mother, who'd once lain in bed
at the brink of dawn, very peaceful.
Very pleasantly, she said, for once
she felt no pain, she heard the birdsong
and knew death was right there if she chose.
It had been a preparation, she thought.
But later I understood: though they were gone,
I didn't want to go to them, there was no other
place to go, Earth's the right place for love.

This world, the living, the mind where
the literal and figurative collude. Not death
where darkness and silence and dust are
only darkness and silence and dust.

Notes

"Staring into the Sun" is in memory of Joshua Keen.

"Come, No Longer Unthinkable" takes its title and opening lines from W. S. Merwin's poem "Finally."

"Heading There" takes its first line and some of its poetic logic from the opening line of "Vrai nom" by Yves Bonnefoy: "Je nommerai désert ce château que tu fus."

"The Morning Will Be Bright, and Wrong" takes its title from Larry Levis's "Gossip in the Village" and is in memory of Jon Appleton. It also alludes to A. R. Ammons's essay "A Poem Is a Walk."

"Poem or Story" is for Rick Barot.

"Grief" borrows from George Herbert's "Prayer (I)."

"Marseille" is for Alec Stone Sweet.

"The Conversion of Paul" quotes and converses with poems by Paul Otremba, Stanley Plumly, and Thom Gunn.

"Over and Above" adapts language from climate photographer Mitch Dobrowner, Henry David Thoreau, and Simone Weil's assertion in *Gravity and Grace* that "Absolutely unmixed attention is prayer."

"All the Little Clocks Wind Down" borrows phrases and gestures from Denis Johnson's poem "Now" as well as quoting from Rainer Maria Rilke's "In the Drawing Room," translated by Edward Snow.

"In Sicily" is indebted to Anthony Hecht's "A Hill" as well as Robert Frost's "Birches."

Acknowledgments

Thank you to the editors where some of these poems originally appeared:

The Academy of American Poets' *Poem-a-Day*: "Staring into the Sun"
The American Poetry Review: "Free Fall," "Who Understands"
Birmingham Poetry Review: "January," "March," "May"
Catamaran: "Go Along"
Cave Wall: "Come, No Longer Unthinkable"
The Georgia Review: "Incantation," "She Kept All These Things and Pondered Them in Her Heart," "The Morning Will Be Bright, and Wrong," "All the Little Clocks Wind Down"
The Literary Review: "November," "December," "Greens and Purples," "The Crows"
The Nation: "iPoem"
New England Review: "Heading There," "The Conversion of Paul," "Poem or Story"
The New York Review of Books: "Marseille"
The New Yorker: "Medium"
Plume: "August," "Rain," "Before"
Poetry London: "In Sicily"
Sierra Magazine: "The Salt Mine"
The Yale Review: "Over and Above"

"March" was reprinted on Poetry Daily, July 2020.

"The Conversion of Paul" was reprinted in *The Best American Poetry 2020*, edited by Paisley Rekdal.

Thank you to Catherine Barnett, Geoffrey Brock, Michael Collier, Sally Keith, Matthew Otremba, Patrick Phillips, and Shirley Stephenson, each of whom read some or all of these poems with care and helped me improve them. And then after that, Jeff Shotts, editor extraordinaire, helped me improve them yet again.

I also wish to thank the John Simon Guggenheim Memorial Foundation, MacDowell, La Maison Dora Maar, Civitella Ranieri, the James Merrill House, and Château de Lavigny, institutions that fostered this work.

Jennifer Grotz is the author of three previous collections of poetry, *Window Left Open*, *The Needle*, and *Cusp*. Also a translator from the French and Polish, her co-translations with Piotr Sommer of Jerzy Ficowski's *Everything I Don't Know* received the PEN Award for Best Book of Poetry in Translation in 2022. A professor at the University of Rochester, she directs the Bread Loaf Writers' Conferences.

The text of *Still Falling* is set in Adobe Caslon.
Book design by Ann Sudmeier. Composition by Bookmobile
Design and Digital Publisher Services, Minneapolis, Minnesota.
Manufactured by Versa Press on acid-free,
30 percent postconsumer wastepaper.